Charles Darwin

Heidi Moore

Heinemann
LIBRARY

www.heinemannlibrary.co.uk
Visit our website to find out more information about **Heinemann** books.

To order:
☎ Phone 44 (0) 1865 888112
🖹 Send a fax to 44 (0) 1865 314091
💻 Visit the Heinemann Bookshop at **www.heinemannlibrary.co.uk** to browse our
catalogue and order online.

Heinemann Library is an imprint of Capstone Global Library Limited, a company incorporated in England and Wales having its registered office at 7 Pilgrim Street, London, EC4V 6LB – Registered company number: 6695582

Heinemann is a registered trademark of Pearson Education Limited, under licence to Capstone Global Library Limited

Text © Capstone Global Library Limited 2008
First published in hardback in 2009
Paperback edition first published in 2010

Edited by Louise Galpine, Rachel Howells, and Adam Miller
Designed by Kimberly R. Miracle and Betsy Wernert
Original illustrations© Pearson Education Ltd
Illustrations by Mapping Specialists, Inc.
Picture research by Mica Brancic and Helen Reilly
Originated by Modern Age
Printed and bound in China by Leo Paper Group

ISBN 978 0 431 04481 1 (hardback)
13 12 11 10 09
10 9 8 7 6 5 4 3 2 1

ISBN 978 0 431 04497 2 (paperback)
14 13 12 11 10
10 9 8 7 6 5 4 3 2 1

British Library Cataloguing in Publication Data
Moore, Heidi, 1976-
Charles Darwin. – (Levelled biographies)
576.8'2'092
A full catalogue record for this book is available from the British Library.

Acknowledgements
We would like to thank the following for permission to reproduce photographs: © AKG Images p. 11; © Alamy p. 8 (Mike Hayward); © Ardea p. 29 (M. Watson); © Cambridge University Library p. 31; © Corbis p. 45, pp. 7, 33, 47 (The Bettmann Archive), 19 (DK Limited), 23 (Tim Graham), 24 (Stuart Westmorland), 27 (Reuters), 35 (Ashley Cooper), 38 (David Ball), 5 (Stapleton Collection), 40 (Frank Lane Picture Agency/Douglas P. Wilson), 42 (Hulton-Deutch Collection), 44, 46 (National Museum of Ethiopia); © Crestock p. 12; © English Heritage Picture Library p. 37; © Fotolia p. 32 (Ecoview); © Heritage Image Library p. 15; © 2007 Photolibrary.com p. 22 (Mark Jones); © Natural History Museum pp. 43-44; © The Bridgeman Art Library pp. 6 (Darwin College, Cambridge, UK), 10 (Private Collection, Ken Welsh), 36 (Down House, Kent, UK); © The National Portrait Gallery p. 17; © The Science Photo Library p. 21 (Tom McHugh).

Cover photograph of Charles Darwin reproduced with permission of ©Corbis (epa/Handout/Richard Milner).

We would like to thank Nancy Harris for her invaluable help in the preparation of this book.

Every effort has been made to contact copyright holders of any material reproduced in this book. Any omissions will be rectified in subsequent printings if notice is given to the publisher.

CONTENTS

Some words are shown in bold, **like this**. You can find out what they mean by looking in the glossary.

THE MAN BEHIND THE THEORY

Billions of years ago, there was no life on Earth. There were landmasses and oceans, but there were no **organisms** (living things). Eventually the first one-celled creatures formed in water. They quickly multiplied and began to populate Earth. Soon these tiny organisms began to mutate (change).

Over time, these **mutations** began to build up. The first organisms gave rise to simple new life-forms that, in turn, gave rise to more complex lifeforms. In a cycle of change that happened time after time, Earth's lifeforms slowly replaced one another. Over hundreds of millions of years, this process gave rise to every life-form on Earth, living or extinct. These include dinosaurs, chimpanzees, oysters, lizards, humans, and more.

Looking for answers

Why does life on Earth keep changing? How do new **species** form? These were some of the questions Charles Darwin sought to answer.

Charles Darwin was a British scientist and **naturalist** who lived in the 1800s. Gathering evidence from the world around him, he began to piece together an explanation of how living things change over time. Darwin's **theory** (explanation) of **evolution** had an enormous impact on science. It changed our understanding of the world and humans' place in it.

What experiences shaped Darwin's famous theory? What was he like as a person? Read on to meet the man behind the theory – Charles Darwin.

Victorian Britain
The period between 1837 and 1901 is called the Victorian **era**. Queen Victoria ruled Great Britain during this time.

The world of Darwin

Charles Darwin (above) lived in the 19th century. During this time important developments were shaping Great Britain and other countries. The **Industrial Revolution** brought new technology that changed the way people lived and worked. Steam engines powered huge ships across vast oceans. Railroads cut through the landscape, allowing people to travel quickly and easily between towns. Work that was once **manual** (done by hand) was now done by machines. This forever changed the way people produced goods.

Naturalist in Training

Charles Robert Darwin was born on 12 February 1809, in Shrewsbury, England. His parents were Susannah Wedgwood and Robert Waring Darwin. Darwin had four sisters and one older brother.

The Darwin family was known throughout England. Darwin's father, Robert, was a wealthy doctor, and Robert Darwin's own father, Erasmus Darwin, was a leading doctor and thinker. His mother's father was Josiah Wedgwood, a leading maker of fine china.

When Charles Darwin was young, people called him Charley. His family lived in Mount House, a large brick house on a hill overlooking the River Severn. Darwin loved fishing in the river. When Darwin was just eight years old, his mother died. After that his older sisters mostly took care of him.

Erasmus Darwin

Charles Darwin's grandfather on his father's side was Erasmus Darwin (above). Erasmus Darwin lived from 1731–1802. He had many talents. He was a doctor, like his son, as well as a **botanist**, a naturalist, and a poet. In his 1794 book, *Zoonomia*, he presented one of the first **theories** of **evolution**, which explained how living things change over time. Erasmus Darwin also believed that all life evolved from one common ancestor. Many of his ideas were far ahead of their time. He often discussed his theories with his grandson, Charley. He had a huge influence on the boy.

Josiah Wedgwood

Charles Darwin's other grandfather was Josiah Wedgwood (1730–1795). Wedgwood's china was known throughout Great Britain and Europe for its beauty and quality. Wedgwood also started the country's first pottery factories and invented new and better ways of making ceramics. Wedgwood china is still popular today.

He later wrote that he was a naughty child. He liked to steal fruit from the orchard next to his house. He would sneak outside and use a long stick to knock peaches and plums off the trees into a large flowerpot.

A budding **naturalist**, Darwin was interested in nature and living things from an early age. He loved looking at plants and enjoyed roaming through Mount House's vast gardens. He also kept collections of insects, minerals, stamps, and coins.

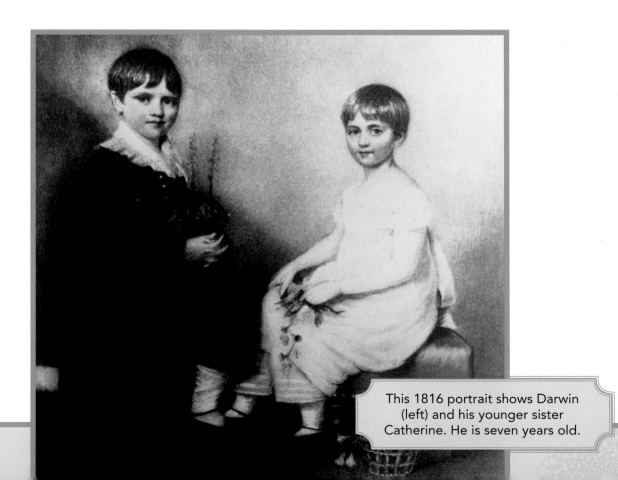

This 1816 portrait shows Darwin (left) and his younger sister Catherine. He is seven years old.

Darwin could still visit his family home (above) after he went away to board at Shrewsbury School.

Early studies

In 1818 Darwin began attending Shrewsbury School, an all-boys boarding school. At a boarding school, students live on site during the school year. Darwin was just nine years old when he went away from home. But the school was close to Mount House, and he visited his family often.

Under the leadership of Samuel Butler, the headmaster, Shrewsbury School mostly taught the classics. Students had to read and memorize many old Greek and Latin texts. Darwin found it boring and did not stand out at school. He especially hated memorizing long passages in Greek. He later wrote that "nothing could have been worse for the development of my mind than Dr Butler's school".

However, Darwin had a quick mind for other subjects. He loved poetry and the plays of William Shakespeare. He also loved nature and science, and he even read chemistry textbooks for fun.

Chemistry experiments

Around 1822 Darwin's older brother Erasmus built a chemistry laboratory in the toolshed outside Mount House. Darwin was his lab assistant. "He [Erasmus] made all the gases and many compounds, and I read with care several books on chemistry," Darwin later wrote. "The subject interested me greatly, and we often used to go on working till rather late at night. This was the best part of my education at school, for it showed me practically the meaning of experimental [hands-on] science."

Pupils at school found out about Darwin's chemistry experiments at home and started teasing him. They gave him the nickname "Gas". At the time it was unusual to do chemistry experiments. Even the headmaster thought Darwin's experiments were a waste of time.

Shrewsbury then and now

Shrewsbury School is one of the oldest, largest, and best-known boarding schools in England. King Edward VI founded the school in 1552. Many famous politicians, writers, and actors have attended the school. In September 2008 Shrewsbury started admitting girls for the first time in its 500-year history!

Medical school

Charles Darwin graduated from Shrewsbury School in 1825. Now 16 years old, he began attending Edinburgh University, where his older brother Erasmus was already studying. The Darwin brothers were following in the footsteps of their father, Robert Darwin, and their grandfather, Erasmus Darwin. They were studying to be doctors.

Edinburgh University had a fine medical school with excellent teachers. But Darwin found most of his courses boring. The only classes he enjoyed were **geology**, the study of rocks and minerals, and **botany**, the study of plants. He also kept up with his childhood collections and began gathering **marine** creatures such as sea slugs and oysters.

Robert Grant

At Edinburgh, Darwin learned **taxidermy**. This involved preparing, stuffing, and mounting dead birds and animals. He also studied with a professor whom he admired, called Robert Grant.

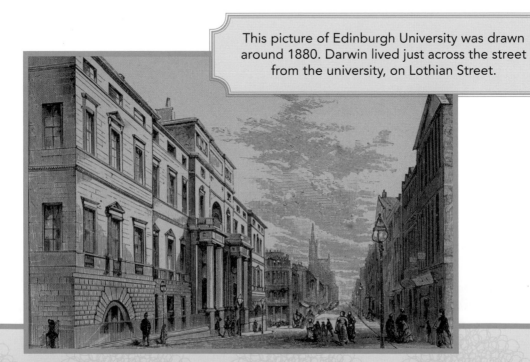

This picture of Edinburgh University was drawn around 1880. Darwin lived just across the street from the university, on Lothian Street.

Grant taught him how to **dissect** marine animals under a microscope. Grant had read Darwin's grandfather's book *Zoonomia* and believed in evolution. Grant also believed, like Darwin's grandfather did, that all animals shared a common ancestor. Grant thought that this ancestor was a marine creature and that life on Earth began in the oceans. Darwin and his professor talked in depth about these ideas and many others.

Although Darwin loved science, he still did not want to be a doctor. He hated studying **anatomy**, the structure of the human body, and surgery made him sick!

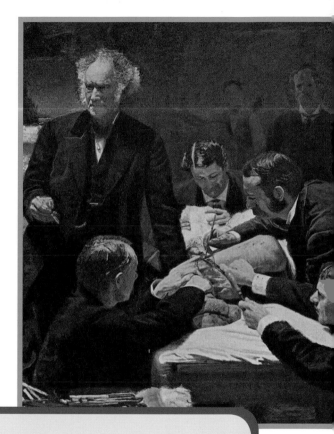

19th-century surgery

In the early 1800s, surgery was extremely risky. Many patients died on the operating table. There was no safe **anaesthesia** to put patients to sleep or to block pain. The painkillers that were available were not very effective or had dangerous side effects.

Patients who survived surgery often died of **infection** afterwards. Before the 1860s, operating rooms were often dirty. Scientists did not know until 1865 that bacteria (germs) caused infection. Soon after, doctors were urged to wash their hands and surgical tools before surgery. Before that, doctors did not understand the importance of keeping things **sterile**. In Darwin's time, surgery was painful, bloody, and dangerous. The picture above shows surgery in progress. It was painted by Thomas Eakins in 1875, and is called *The Gross Clinic*.

Cambridge

By 1827 things had not changed – Darwin still hated medical school. He did not put much effort into his classes at Edinburgh University, so his father decided to transfer him to Christ's College, Cambridge. His father thought it would be better for a young naturalist. The course would not be as difficult. Darwin would have plenty of time to pursue botany and science in his free time while studying **theology** (religion) at the university. In 1828 Darwin started preparing for a career in the church.

Darwin lived at Fitzwilliam Street in Cambridge. This modern photograph shows what his lodgings look like now.

Beetle collecting

At Cambridge, Darwin spent time with his second cousin William Darwin Fox, who also studied there. Fox was an enthusiastic beetle collector, and he shared his hobby with Darwin. Together the cousins took long walks in the countryside, collecting beetle **specimens**. Darwin even sent away for a magazine about insects. At one point he sent in records of some fresh specimens he had collected, and the magazine published illustrations of them. Darwin was thrilled.

"No pursuit at Cambridge was followed with nearly so much eagerness or gave me so much pleasure as collecting beetles," Darwin later wrote. "It was the mere passion for collecting, for I did not dissect them and rarely compared the external characteristics [outside features] with published descriptions."

University success

Darwin did well at Cambridge, though he did not always attend class. He did, however, take the college's only botany course three times. This caught the attention of the botany professor, John Stevens Henslow. Henslow became Darwin's teacher and **mentor**. Darwin later said that Henslow "influenced my career more than any other".

Another Cambridge professor, the geology teacher Adam Sedgwick, also took an interest in Darwin. Sedgwick took Darwin on a trip to Wales during the summer of 1831. He showed Darwin how to collect geology specimens, such as rocks and soil samples. This gave Darwin important firsthand experience collecting data and specimens in the field.

Darwin graduated from Cambridge in 1831. He was tenth in his class. Now he had a degree and some important field experience. He was ready for his next adventure!

Voyage of the Beagle

After graduating from Cambridge, Darwin began planning a trip to the Canary Islands, off the northwest coast of Africa. But he never made it there. Instead, he received an invitation for a different voyage, one that would change his life forever.

When he returned from Wales in August 1831, he received a letter from his Cambridge **mentor**, John Stevens Henslow, about an upcoming sea voyage. The HMS *Beagle* was to **circumnavigate** the world as it charted coastlines for mapmaking. Better maps would make it easier to trade with different parts of the world. The captain, a 26-year-old sailor named Robert FitzRoy, needed a **naturalist** to sail with him and collect plant and animal **specimens**.

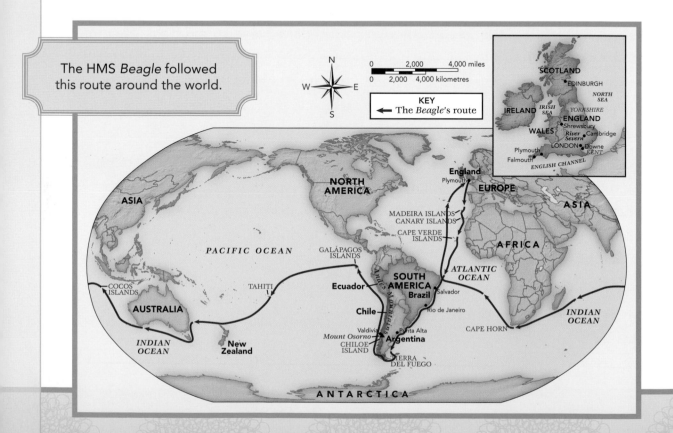

The HMS *Beagle* followed this route around the world.

At first Darwin's strict father did not approve. He told his son the trip sounded risky and dangerous. Instead, he thought Darwin should settle down and join the church. However, his father gave him one chance to prove him wrong. If Darwin could find one "man of common sense" who thought the trip was a good idea, his father would grant him permission.

Finally, in early September, Darwin's uncle, Josiah Wedgwood, son of the china-maker, sent a letter urging Darwin's father to send Darwin on the voyage. Darwin's father respected Wedgwood very much, so he agreed.

Now Darwin had less than a month to pack for his journey around the world. Before he left, he travelled to London Zoo to learn how to preserve and store plant and animal specimens. He would need to keep his specimens safe during the long journey. At least he already knew about **taxidermy** from his time at Edinburgh University.

Darwin would encounter many different cultures on his long voyage. He came across this Patagonian man around 1833. Patagonia is a large area that spans southern Argentina and Chile, South America.

What's in a name?

In Great Britain, ship names often start with the letters "HMS". This stands for "her **majesty's** ship" or "his majesty's ship". "Her majesty" and "his majesty" are titles of respect for the queen or king. The ships were named this way because they sailed in the service of the king or queen who ruled at the time.

First stop

The HMS *Beagle* was to sail first to Tierra del Fuego, at the southern tip of South America. There, Captain FitzRoy would survey the coastline while Darwin collected specimens to bring back to England to study.

Life aboard the ship

They set sail from Plymouth on 27 December 1831. The *Beagle* was a small ship for such a long journey – only 27 metres (90 feet) long. Darwin shared a cabin that was 3.4 by 3 metres (11 by 10 feet) long with two other men. It was about the size of a small bedroom. Shelves holding dozens of books lined one cabin wall. Darwin brought along the books to help him understand the **geology** and **botany** of the areas he was to visit. At night he slept in a hammock hung just half a metre (2 feet) from the ceiling.

The journey was rough as the ship travelled over choppy water, and Darwin was seasick from the start. He later wrote, "The misery I endured from seasickness is far beyond what I ever guessed at."

Land of fire

Tierra del Fuego is a group of islands called an **archipelago**, shared by Chile and Argentina. The name means "Land of Fire" in Spanish. The 16th-century explorer Ferdinand Magellan named the area for the locals' bonfires he saw when he landed there.

The work of geologist Charles Lyell had a strong influence on Darwin.

A changing Earth

Perhaps the most important book Darwin brought on the voyage was Charles Lyell's *Principles of Geology*, published in 1830. In it Lyell argued that Earth was much older than people thought and was changing steadily over time. He argued that Earth's surface had shifted and moved over millions of years. Sea levels had risen and fallen.

Lyell's **theory** of a changing Earth went against what most people believed at the time. Most of 19th-century Europe believed the Bible's version of creation and thought Earth was just 6,000 years old. Lyell sought to prove that it was much older – millions of years old – and that there was clear evidence of a changing Earth. "The present is the key to the past," Lyell wrote. This idea guided Darwin's thinking on his journey.

Rising land, falling land

In January 1832 the ship neared the Canary Islands, off the northwest coast of Africa. But Darwin did not get to set foot on the islands he had long dreamed of visiting. There had been an outbreak of **cholera** back in England. The islanders feared catching the disease from the English sailors, so the ship was forbidden to land.

Captain FitzRoy sailed on, heading south along the west coast of Africa to the Cape Verde Islands. Darwin was amazed by everything he saw at sea, including an octopus that could change colour and shoot out dark ink. "A child with a new toy could not have been more delighted," Captain FitzRoy said about Darwin.

Darwin went ashore and made a remarkable discovery. He noticed a white band of oyster shells high on a cliff face about 14 metres (45 feet) above sea level. Darwin wondered what this could mean. How did these oyster shells get to be on dry land?

Darwin began thinking that Charles Lyell's book might be right. Slowly, over long periods of time, the land was falling in some places and rising in others. At one time the ocean must have been high enough to cover most of the Cape Verde Islands. Over time the land rose, exposing areas of rock that were previously underwater. The oysters, once underwater, were pushed up out of the water and now lay in dry rock.

Darwin found fossilized shells like these embedded in rock high on a cliff.

This was an incredible discovery. Nothing would look the same to Darwin after this. He began questioning everything he knew about the history of Earth and life on it. Perhaps he would find even more evidence of a changing Earth.

In February the *Beagle* left the Cape Verde Islands and sailed on towards Brazil, crossing the Equator on 16 February. Now it was on to South America!

In Darwin's words

"It then first dawned on me that I might perhaps write a book on the geology of the various countries visited, and this made me thrill with delight."

Charles Darwin,
Cape Verde Islands,
January 1832

Exploring South America

In late February 1832, the HMS *Beagle* dropped anchor in Salvador, Brazil. The ship had finally made it to South America! Darwin explored the rainforest and was amazed by the **diversity** of plant and animal life within it.

In the city, Darwin witnessed slavery up close for the first time. He saw how badly the enslaved African people were treated. Darwin tried to discuss the cruelty of slavery with Captain FitzRoy, but he discovered that FitzRoy supported the slave trade. The two men got into a huge argument. Darwin strongly believed that it was wrong to treat humans as property. Eventually, Darwin and FitzRoy made up, but Darwin never forgot what he had witnessed in Brazil.

Fossil hunting

After leaving Salvador, the ship continued sailing south. Darwin spent several months exploring the area around Rio de Janeiro in Brazil. He hunted for specimens amid buzzing cicadas (insects with long wings – the males make a droning noise) and brightly coloured tree frogs. "It was impossible to wish for anything more delightful than thus to spend some weeks in so magnificent a country," Darwin later wrote.

From there the *Beagle* continued its journey south to Argentina, where Darwin made some of his most important **fossil** discoveries. In a cliff at Punta Alta, he found huge fossilized bones of strange-looking animals. He thought they were ancient rhinoceroses and **mastodons**. Later, Darwin would discover that they were the remains of a giant ground **sloth** and an **armadillo** the size of a cow.

Darwin wondered what caused these giant animals to become extinct. There was little vegetation in the area to support such large creatures. What could have happened? Could the plant life have disappeared over thousands of years, causing these animals to slowly die out?

Darwin discovered fossils of large extinct animals similar to this giant ground sloth in Argentina.

Charles Darwin,
Punta Alta, Argentina,
October/November 1832

In Darwin's words

"I have been wonderfully lucky with fossil bones. Some of the animals must have been of great dimensions; I am almost sure that many of them are quite new."

THE RETURN JOURNEY

The voyage was supposed to last just two years, but already two and a half years had passed at sea. In June 1834 the HMS *Beagle* finally rounded Cape Horn, at the southern tip of South America. Now it set sail in the Pacific Ocean on the second half of its attempt to **circumnavigate** Earth.

Changing landforms

In July 1834 the ship reached Chile. In August Darwin headed inland to explore the Andes Mountains. There he discovered shells in dry rock far above high tide. This was similar to what he had seen on the Cape Verde Islands, off Africa's coast. He began to understand that the western side of South America was rising. But what could cause such dramatic changes on Earth's surface?

An event in January 1835 gave him one idea. Chile's Mount Osorno erupted. Perhaps, Darwin thought, powerful volcanoes spewing molten rock could create new landforms. An earthquake in Valdivia, Chile, a month later gave him another explanation. Surely, many such actions over millions of years could change Earth's surface. Both of these acts of nature supported Charles Lyell's **theory**. Earth was indeed changing over time.

Fever

Darwin came down with a terrible fever in August 1834 in the Andes. For the rest of his life he would suffer from terrible headaches and stomachaches that might have been caused by this unknown illness.

The Galapagos Islands

Darwin spent several months exploring the west coast of South America, including Peru and Ecuador. Finally, the *Beagle* dropped anchor at the Galapagos Islands, off the coast of Ecuador.

These hot, volcanic islands swarmed with life. Giant tortoises and **marine** iguanas crawled on the black, rocky land. Many **species** of birds made their home there. Darwin noted the unusual birds he saw on each island and collected some **specimens**. He did not know it at the time, but these birds would give him an important clue as to how animals **adapted** to their environment.

The giant land tortoise is native to the Galapagos Islands.

Change over time

By late 1835 the crew of the HMS *Beagle* was eager to return home. But the ship would still make stops in Tahiti, New Zealand, and Australia. At each stop, Darwin gathered specimens for his now enormous collection. For years he had been shipping specimens home to England in batches.

In April 1836 the ship dropped anchor in the Cocos Islands, in the Indian Ocean. There Darwin saw the remains of **coral reefs** atop mountains. He had already begun to understand coral reef formation. Coral reefs, he thought, must grow on sinking mountain rims. He had pieced this together from observation. Now here was more support for his view. This evidence also supported Lyell's theory of a changing Earth. By now Darwin had no doubt that Lyell was right.

Colourful coral reefs grow in warm tropical waters.

Mystery of mysteries

Soon Darwin turned to a second problem: Where did new animal species come from? Darwin called this the "mystery of mysteries". He already knew that some species died out and others took their place. But what, he wondered, caused this to happen? And how did new species come about?

As the ship neared Europe, Darwin completed his diary of the journey. It was 770 pages long. He also had over 1,500 pages of field notes. He had page after page on the **geology** of each place he had visited. He also had specimens of more than 1,500 plant and animal species, preserved for later study.

In October 1836 the weary crew of the HMS *Beagle* finally returned to England. They had been at sea nearly five years. During that time, Darwin spent only 18 months total on board the ship. Most of the time he was off exploring land, where he gathered specimens and witnessed acts of nature such as earthquakes and volcanic eruptions.

Based on these experiences, Darwin began to give shape to theories that would change science forever. He now had enough specimens to study and enough ideas to think about for decades.

Charles Darwin,
Falmouth, England,
2 October 1836

In Darwin's words
"I reached home late last night. My head is quite confused with so much delight."

Looking for answers

The HMS *Beagle* voyage changed Darwin's life forever. He left England a young **theology** student who was about to join the church. He returned a skilled **naturalist** with a vast collection of specimens. His collection contained hundreds of plant and animal species that no one in Britain or Europe had ever seen before. It was an amazing achievement for such a young man.

Darwin was now 27 years old. He had come a long way from being teased by his classmates and called "Gas" for his love of science. Now he was a real scientist who had made important discoveries. He gave talks about coral reef formation and the geology of the Andes Mountains, and many people came to hear him. He also published *Journal and Remarks* (*The voyage of the* Beagle), a book of his *Beagle* diaries. It sold thousands of copies and brought him fame in London and beyond.

Now he applied for, and received, a government **grant**. He used the grant money to hire science experts to examine his specimens and tell him exactly what he had collected. Then Darwin would publish a book of their findings.

A new honour

In January 1837 the Geological Society of London elected Darwin a member. Founded in 1807, it is the world's oldest geology club. Its members meet to share ideas about geology and Earth science. In 1838 Darwin became the group's secretary.

Builders in Cuzco, Peru discovered the fossilized remains of a giant armadillo, like the type Darwin found in Argentina.

An expert in **anatomy** examined the huge **fossils** from Argentina. He told Darwin that they were the remains of large extinct **armadillos**, anteaters, and **sloths**. This surprised Darwin. He wondered what caused these giant animals to die out.

The birds from the Galapagos were perhaps strangest of all. They were not different species of birds, as Darwin had thought. Instead, they were all finches. Each island had its own type of finch with slight **variations**, or differences, that set it apart from the finches on other islands. Darwin wondered what caused this. Could the finches have adapted to slightly different conditions on each island?

Darwin turned back to his "mystery of mysteries", finding out where new species come from.

A Galapagos finch from Santa Cruz Island perches on a flower.

THEORY OF EVOLUTION

Back home in London, Darwin began looking into the **origin** (beginning) of **species**. He thought back to Charles Lyell's **theory** of a changing Earth. If Earth could change over time, he thought, why not animals? Maybe species did not stay the same forever. But how – and why – did **evolution** occur?

The fossil record

The **fossil record** gave Darwin and other scientists many clues into the history of Earth and its creatures. Scientists dug deep in the ground and discovered fossils of species that had lived long ago. In each layer of earth, they found the remains of very different types of animals. This proved that different species lived on Earth at different ages. Over time certain species died out and new ones took their place. But how did these new species come about?

Darwin's own fossils gave him some important clues. The fossils he found in South America looked like giant versions of the live **armadillos**, anteaters, and **sloths** he had seen there. Could these smaller animals have replaced their extinct ancestors? Perhaps the giant animals died out as a result of some change in their environment. Then new animals better suited to the environment took their place. This would explain why evolution took place, but *how* did it take place?

Darwin thought about his Galapagos **specimens**. Each island had its own group of finches with slight **variations** that set them apart from their neighbours. Perhaps these groups were on their way to becoming different species. At the least they were proof that species were changing – not unchanging, as most people believed.

Perhaps, Darwin thought, species could evolve into new species. Remote spots like islands would be perfect places for this to happen. Away from others of their kind, species would **adapt** to their surroundings over time and start the slow march to becoming new species.

With these ideas in mind, Darwin began working on an exciting new theory. Like his grandfather, Erasmus Darwin, he called it a theory of transmutation. The word *transmutation* means "a change in form". Today people call it evolution.

Galapagos species, such as this marine iguana, gave Darwin clues about the process of evolution.

Looking at evolution

Between 1837 and 1839, Darwin worked on his theory of transmutation. As time went on, he found more and more evidence to support it. This made him excited, but also worried. Evolution went against the view of species as **stable** and unchanging. This was what most people in the Western world believed at the time and what the Bible taught. Darwin wrote in his notebook, "If species were not stable, but could give rise to new species, everything in natural history would be seen in a new light."

Model of evolution: a branching tree

Before long, Darwin sketched out one possible model of transmutation – a tree with many branches. Among the few scientists at the time who believed in evolution, most thought it happened only in an upward direction. Their model was a ladder. As a species evolved, they argued, it climbed up the ladder towards its ideal (best) form.

Darwin believed evolution did not happen so neatly. The Galapagos finches, for example, were branching off in many directions at once. There did not seem to be one ideal form of finch. Instead, each island supported one type of finch with a unique set of variations. One group was not better than the others, just different. Each group was better suited to its own environment.

Darwin found support for his branching tree model in tortoise specimens from the Galapagos. Tortoises on one island had shells that were higher in front. This made it easier for them to raise their heads to eat tall cactus plants. Tortoises on another island had dome-shaped shells. They could not raise their necks much at all – they did not need to! They fed on plants on the ground.

The shell shapes were probably **adaptations**, Darwin thought. A tortoise with a shell shape suited to its island would get enough food. It would survive. A tortoise with a poor shell shape for its island would die out. Darwin called this process **natural selection**. It means that nature selects certain variations in species. Over time only animals with helpful variations survive.

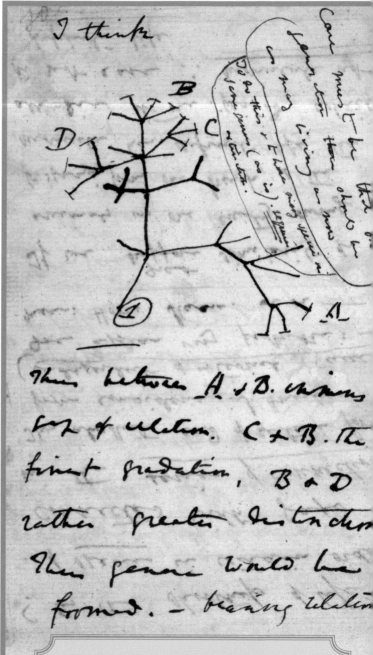

Darwin drew this in his notebook around July 1837. It shows his first known sketch of an evolutionary tree.

Natural and forced selection

Charles Darwin was not the first scientist to offer a theory of evolution. His grandfather Erasmus Darwin had formed his own theory nearly 50 years earlier. However, the idea of natural selection was Darwin's alone and was a huge achievement. Before Darwin, no one had worked out how evolution took place.

Darwin was now certain that animals evolved through natural selection. He found evidence in the world around him. Even animal breeding supported his theory. Breeders selected animals with helpful characteristics (features). Then they bred (mated) them to pass on these characteristics.

For example, dog breeders bred certain dogs to be fast. They bred others to be good at tracking scents. Over time only puppies with those traits were born. The breeders were able to change the dog species! Darwin called this practice artificial (forced) selection. Everywhere Darwin looked, he saw examples of evolution in progress.

Racing dogs like these are bred for speed.

Thomas Malthus

Thomas Malthus (right) lived from 1766–1834. He was an English economist who studied population growth. He believed that society should restrict family size to eliminate poverty and starvation.

Survival of the fittest

In September 1838 Darwin read an essay by the **economist** Thomas Malthus. It said that the limited food supply limits population size. In other words, populations produce more offspring than can survive with the available food, so members must compete for food. Those who do not find enough food will die out. This is nature's way of keeping the population at a reasonable size.

Darwin latched onto this idea of **competition**. Darwin thought that competition for resources is what drives evolution. Animals with helpful variations are able to get enough food. These animals survive to reproduce, passing on their helpful traits. Over time those without the helpful variations die out. The variation can be a small thing, such as eye shape or colour, or something more major, such as size.

He called this process survival of the fittest. It means that animals that are best suited to their environment survive. This idea became key to Darwin's theory.

Questioning beliefs

As early as September 1837, Darwin began to suffer from an illness. No one is certain what it was. It might have been the illness he caught in Chile. Or perhaps he was simply worried about his work on evolution. He knew that some people would think his theory was wrong.

After all, Darwin's theory went against widely held beliefs. The idea that Earth was changing would have been upsetting to most people in early 19th-century Britain and elsewhere in the Western world. They believed the world had a certain order – it was stable and unchanging. Evolution went against those beliefs. It said that the world and its species were constantly changing.

Common ancestor

Most people at the time believed that humans were "above" animals, but Darwin noted similarities across many species. He began to believe that all animals, including humans, were related.

The structure of animal limbs pointed to a common ancestor. Darwin looked at the skeletons of humans, bats, and porpoises. He found certain similarities. Human hands, bat wings, and porpoise fins share a similar structure. The difference is that each one is adapted to its special purpose – human hands to grasp, bat wings to fly, and porpoise fins to swim. Darwin noted how these limbs seemed related. He reasoned that different species must have branched off long ago from a common (shared) ancestor.

Passing on characteristics

One mystery remained. How do animals pass on their traits to their offspring? Darwin was not sure, so he came up with an idea. Perhaps animals have tiny pieces of material in their sex organs. Darwin called these pieces gemmules. Animals must make copies of their gemmules and pass them on to their offspring, he thought. He called this process pangenesis.

Many years later, scientists would confirm his theory. Today scientists call these gemmules **genes**. Genes are tiny strings of code that parents pass on to their offspring. Genes determine an animal's characteristics, such as size, eye colour, and skin type.

Genes allow male peacocks to develop colourful plumage to attract female mates.

A NEW CHAPTER

Darwin would continue to work on his **theory** of **evolution** by **natural selection** for 20 more years. It was almost complete by early 1839.

Now 29 years old, Darwin began thinking about marriage, yet he was afraid that it might take time away from his work as a **naturalist** and scientist. He decided to make a list of the pros and cons of getting married. On the con side, he wrote "less money for books" and "terrible loss of time". On the pro side, he wrote "constant companion", "friend in old age", and "children". In the end, the pro side won out. He decided he would find a wife and get married.

He wasted little time. On 29 January 1839, Darwin married his cousin Emma Wedgwood. At the time it was normal to marry one's cousin. Emma and Charles Darwin were a great match. They loved and supported each other for the rest of their lives.

Emma Darwin became a source of comfort and support for Charles Darwin.

Emma Darwin

Emma Wedgwood (1808–1896) was Darwin's wife and first cousin. They had the same grandfather—Josiah Wedgwood, the famous china-maker. Like her husband, Emma Darwin loved outdoor sports. In her youth she studied piano in Paris with the famous pianist Frederic Chopin.

However, Emma Darwin did not share her husband's views on evolution. When Darwin told his young wife about his theory, she was shocked and upset. Darwin knew then that his fears were correct. Society was not ready to hear his ideas about evolution and natural selection. For many years, the fear of making people angry and upset kept Darwin from sharing his theory with the world.

In 1842 the Darwins moved to the village of Downe, in Kent, just outside London. Their home, Down House, was in a spot far from the rest of the village. In the country there was plenty of time for taking long walks and enjoying the outdoors. Charles and Emma Darwin went on to have 10 children at Down House.

William Darwin was the first of Charles and Emma Darwin's 10 children.

Life at Down House

In the early 1840s, Darwin settled down at Down House with his wife and children. Darwin once wrote that the house was "at the extreme edge of the world", but it was really just 26 kilometres (16 miles) from the centre of London. Darwin may have exaggerated in order to show that he felt far from the worries and stresses of city life when at Down House.

At Down House, away from the bustle of city life, Darwin could focus on his work without interruption.

In 1842 Darwin worked on his first paper on his theory of evolution by natural selection. The first draft was 35 pages long. In 1844 he went back to the article and made it longer, but he still did not send it out for publication. He told his wife, Emma, to send it out to publishers if he died.

Darwin might have meant to keep his theory secret until after his death. He even told his friend Joseph Hooker, a fellow scientist, that discussing his belief in evolution was "like confessing a murder". He was afraid of what society might think of him if he shared his views, so he stayed silent.

At Down House, Darwin led a quiet life with his family. He kept a very normal schedule. He took walks, napped, and read at the same time every day. He also kept up with his scientific work. He raised honeybees in the garden to study. In a large greenhouse he grew orchids and other unusual plants, planting multiple generations and studying their traits. He observed that plant **species** also passed along helpful **variations** such as beauty (to attract insects). Darwin passed long hours in his study, surrounded by his **geology** books and notebooks on evolution.

In the 1840s, several works based on Darwin's *Beagle* voyage discoveries were published. Darwin also completed a book on **coral reef** formation and another one on South American geology. By 1846 Darwin had achieved fame as a leading geologist. He also belonged to the Royal Society of London.

Royal Society

The Royal Society is a group of British scientists that was founded in 1660. The group's aim is to advance science. Darwin became a member of the society in January 1839.

A major scientific award

By 1854 Darwin had published a major study on barnacles. A barnacle is a **marine** creature with a hard, plated shell. Adult barnacles attach themselves to rocks, ships, and even whales. A year earlier, the Royal Society had awarded Darwin its Royal Medal for the study. The award brought attention to his work in biology. Now Darwin was seen as an expert in almost every branch of science.

Darwin's long study of barnacles taught him about variation within species.

Finishing touches

In 1854 Darwin put the final touches to his theory of evolution. To do this, he borrowed an idea from his grandfather Josiah Wedgwood, the china-maker. In pottery factories and other workplaces, there is division of labour. Different people perform different tasks. In crowded places like these, people have to **specialize**.

Darwin believed that this was the same in nature. Members of a species must specialize to survive. They must take over different parts of a **habitat** to find enough food. This was why, in some places, species quickly branched off into different groups. This supported Darwin's tree model of evolution.

Changing Britain

By the mid-1850s, things were different in Britain. Scientists were discovering new things, and getting essays published. Darwin believed it might be time to share his ideas.

The scientist T. H. Huxley visited Down House in 1856 and learned of Darwin's theory of evolution. Huxley urged him to share his theory. Charles Lyell, whose book Darwin read on the *Beagle* voyage, also visited Darwin and supported his work.

Later that year, Darwin began a major work entitled *Natural Selection*. Finally he was preparing to share his theory with the world!

T. H. Huxley

Thomas Henry Huxley (1825–1895) was a famous biologist. He was called a freethinker because he spoke out against common beliefs of the time. For example, Huxley argued that the **fossil record** showed that humans were not at the centre of creation. Huxley became a close friend of Darwin's. His wife, Nettie, became very good friends with Darwin's wife, Emma.

Alfred Russel Wallace was a naturalist who developed a theory of natural selection at the same time as Darwin. This is him at the age of 77.

Sharing the discovery

As Darwin was working on his three-part book, *Natural Selection*, some bad news reached him. On 18 June 1858, he received a letter from another British naturalist. His name was Alfred Russel Wallace. The letter described the man's theory of change over time.

This was exactly like Darwin's theory of transmutation, or evolution! Wallace even drew from the work of the **economist** Thomas Malthus, just as Darwin did. Wallace's theory also stated that **competition** for resources drives evolution. Darwin knew he had to act fast or everything he had worked on for so long would be for nothing.

Darwin and Wallace decided to announce their discovery together on 1 July 1858. However, Darwin was not there to read his theory. He was away, ill and mourning the death of his youngest son, Charles Waring Darwin, from **scarlet fever**. He left it to his good friends, the scientists Charles Lyell and Joseph Hooker. They read a short essay Darwin had taken from the three-part book on which he was working.

Then Darwin began work on a book-length version of the essay. He called it *On the Origin of Species by Means of Natural Selection*. It was published on 24 November 1859, and it sold out the first day.

Origin of Species shocked many people, but by then many important scientists supported Darwin's work. Huxley, for one, was prepared to defend Darwin's theories with all his power. He wrote in a letter to Darwin dated 23 November 1859, "I am sharpening up my claws and beak in readiness."

By now Darwin was sicker than ever. In late 1859 he travelled to the Yorkshire Moors in northern England to relax. He was terribly afraid of how people would react to his book. He told friends he felt like he was "living in Hell".

In fact, he was right to be worried. The powerful Church of England attacked the book because it did not support the Bible's view of creation. However, Darwin's friends and fellow scientists were prepared. Huxley, Lyell, Hooker, and others defended Darwin and provided evidence to support Darwin's theory.

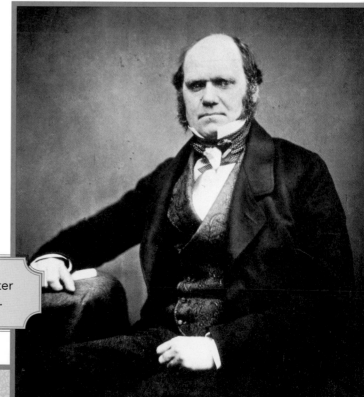

Darwin at the age of 51, a year after *Origin of Species* was published.

THE THEORY TAKES HOLD

By 1860 almost everybody was talking about Darwin's book. It sold tens of thousands of copies in Britain and elsewhere. Most people were not as upset by it as Darwin had feared. Others doubted and debated its ideas.

Many readers quickly saw what the **theory** meant for humans. If all **species** experienced **evolution**, then so did humans. Did that mean humans **descended** from apes, as some scientists at the time claimed? Darwin had left this out of the book on purpose. He knew it would be difficult for people to accept. Humankind has made such amazing achievements, people argued. How could humans be lowly animals?

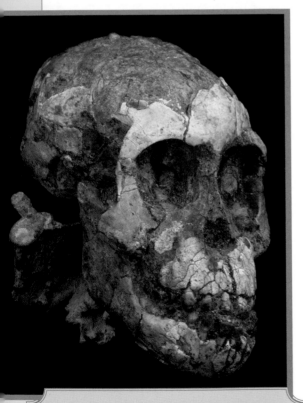

This fossilized skull of a hominid, (early human) reveals important information about human evolution.

Nothing to do but keep working

The late 1860s were a difficult time for Darwin. He was now the most famous scientist of his time, but he was ill for long periods. One month he vomited for 27 days in a row!

Still, he managed to produce more important works. In 1862 he wrote a book about orchids. In it he argued that the flower's beauty was an **adaptation**. Its unusual shape attracted insects for pollination. This book gave more support to his theory of evolution by **natural selection**. In 1864 Darwin won the Royal Society's biggest honour, the Copley Medal.

Cartoons at the time mocked Darwin's view that humans descended from apes.

In 1871 Darwin completed *The Descent of Man*, a book about human evolution. In it Darwin tackled human **origins** among the apes. The book also discussed sexual selection – the idea that animals select mates based on certain traits. Female peacocks, for example, choose males with colourful plumage. Humans practise sexual selection, too, Darwin wrote, but different societies value different traits.

People reacted strongly to the book. Cartoons in newspapers attacked the idea that humans have ape-like ancestors. But T. H. Huxley and many other important scientists backed Darwin and shared evidence from the **fossil record** that supported his claims.

From 1876 to 1881, Darwin wrote his **autobiography**. It looked back at a life filled with exciting discoveries and the comforts of a loving family. The book was not meant for anyone but his family to see. As usual Darwin wanted to keep it to himself.

After Darwin

Charles Darwin died on 19 April 1882, at the age of 73. Newspapers announced the death of the scientist with the "sweet and gentle nature".

Although Darwin was not religious, he was buried in Westminster Abbey, the most famous church in London. Many British kings, queens, and writers are also buried there. Leading scientists and church members attended his funeral.

His work lives on

Darwin's theory of evolution changed science forever. Since Darwin's time, scientists have uncovered more and more evidence to support it. New tools to date **fossils** have revealed exciting information about evolution that was previously hidden in the fossil record.

Scientists have also unlocked **DNA**, the code that forms the basis of all life. DNA contains the genetic instructions used in the functioning of all living things. Most similarities among species are due to shared DNA. By studying DNA, scientists have learned that humans' closest living relatives are chimpanzees.

Darwin's theory also has helped scientists cure deadly diseases. Certain bacteria that cause disease are able to evolve. So scientists must keep developing new **antibiotics** to fight the bacteria. This important work saves millions of lives each year.

This photograph of Darwin was taken one year before he died.

The debate continues

From the time *Origin of Species* first came out, some people have argued against Darwin's theory. Some believe it goes against the Bible's view of creation. However, many people believe in both religion and evolution.

The debate over evolution continues today. Some people want to stop schools from teaching it. However, Darwin's theory remains widely accepted by scientists. It is important for pupils to learn, as it is the basis of all science today.

Is evolution a fact?

Evolution is a scientific theory. What is a theory? Many people think the word *theory* means "a guess", but that is not true in science. A theory is a statement about the natural world that is supported by evidence. Theories can include facts and laws. Scientific theories can also be tested. The more tests a theory passes, the stronger it is.

Darwin's theory of evolution has passed thousands of tests over more than 100 years. As scientists learn more and more about life on Earth, Darwin's theory continues to hold true.

In 1925, in Tennessee, USA, John Scopes, a biology teacher, was found guilty of teaching evolution. This became known as the Scopes monkey trial. The courtroom is pictured below.

TIMELINES

Charles Darwin's life

1809 Born in Shrewsbury, England, on 12 February

1818 Leaves home to attend Shrewsbury School

1822 Performs chemistry experiments in a lab outside Mount House, earning him the nickname "Gas"

1825 Graduates from Shrewsbury. Begins medical school at Edinburgh University.

1827 Leaves Edinburgh

1828 Begins studying **theology** (religion) at Christ's College, Cambridge

1831 Graduates from Cambridge.
Travels to Wales with **geology** professor Adam Sedgwick.
HMS *Beagle* sets sail from Plymouth, England, on 27 December.

1832 Ship crosses Equator on 16 February

1834 *Beagle* rounds Cape Horn in June to begin second half of voyage. In August, Darwin leaves ship to explore Andes mountain range.

1835 Darwin witnesses eruption of Mount Osorno, Chile, in January. Sees the destruction caused by earthquake in Valdivia, Chile, in February.

1836 *Beagle* arrives back in England on 2 October

1837 Geological Society of London elects Darwin a member. He begins work on **theory** of transmutation (**evolution**). His illness begins.

1838 Darwin becomes secretary of the Geological Society

1839	His theory of evolution is nearly complete. Marries first cousin Emma Wedgwood on 29 January. Becomes member of the Royal Society of London.
1842	Emma and Charles Darwin move to the village of Downe, Kent. Darwin writes first essay on theory of evolution by **natural selection**.
1844	Darwin expands essay on evolution
MID-1840S	Publishes work on **coral reef** formation and geology of the Andes Mountains
1852–1854	Completes major study on barnacles. Wins the Royal Society of London's Royal Medal for study.
1854	Completes theory of evolution
1856	Scientist T. H. Huxley visits Down House and urges Darwin to publish his evolution theory. Darwin begins work on the three-volume *Natural Selection*.
1858	Darwin discovers Alfred Russel Wallace has own theory of evolution on 18 June. Charles Lyell and Joseph Hooker read Darwin's paper on evolution at Linnean Society on 1 July.
1859	Publishes *On the Origin of Species by Means of Natural Selection*. It sells out on its first day.
1860	Tens of thousands of copies of *Origin of Species* are sold
1864	Darwin wins the Royal Society's biggest honour, the Copley Medal
1871	Publishes *The Descent of Man*
1881	Darwin completes his **autobiography**
1882	Dies of a heart attack on 19 April and is later buried in Westminster Abbey

World timeline

5 TO 7 MILLION YEARS AGO
Humans and chimpanzees branch off from common ancestor.

100,000 TO 150,000 YEARS AGO
Modern humans' earliest ancestors living in Africa

1750–1830 **Industrial revolution** transforms Great Britain

1794 Erasmus Darwin publishes *Zoonomia*, presenting his theory of evolution

1798 **Economist** Thomas Malthus publishes *Essay on the Principle of Population*

1837 Victorian **era** begins. Queen Victoria reigns.

1838 Darwin first reads Malthus's eassay on population growth

1860 Church of England leader Samuel Wilberforce attacks Darwin's theory. T. H. Huxley and Joseph Hooker support Darwin's work.

1863 T. H. Huxley writes *Evidence as to Man's Place in Nature*, a book on human descent from apes

1864 The French Academy of Sciences accepts chemist Louis Pasteur's discovery that bacteria (germs) cause disease

1869 Swiss physician Friedrich Miescher discovers **DNA**

1870   English surgeon Joseph Lister discovers the importance of **sterile** surgery, urging doctors to wash their hands and clean surgical tools

1901   Victorian era ends with Queen Victoria's death

1925   Scopes monkey trial makes it illegal to teach evolution in schools in Tennessee, USA

1948   U.S. Supreme Court bans religion in public schools

1953   U.S. biologist James Watson and English biologist Francis Crick discover structure of DNA, drawing on the work of English biologist Rosalind Franklin

1955   Jonas Salk develops vaccine against the spinal disease polio

1960s   Tennessee repeals (removes) law against teaching evolution in schools

1999–present   Several school boards rule that teachers must discuss intelligent design (based on Biblical creation) in addition to evolution. In some cases, teachers and parents challenge the school boards in court.

2003   Human Genome Project is completed. It identifies all 20,000 to 25,000 **genes** in human DNA.

GLOSSARY

adapt change to fit in with one's surroundings. Over time animals adapt to their environment.

adaptation change that helps a living thing fit in with its surroundings. The giraffe's long neck is an adaptation to eating leaves high up on trees.

anaesthesia medicine given to block pain or put a patient to sleep. Patients are often given anaesthesia before surgery.

anatomy study of the structure of humans and other living things

antibiotic substance developed to kill certain types of bacteria

archipelago group of islands. Tierra del Fuego is an archipelago in South America.

armadillo burrowing mammal with hard, bony plates covering its body like armour. Armadillos live in South America and the warm southwestern United States.

autobiography book about a person's life written by that person. Darwin wrote his autobiography between 1876 and 1881.

botanist person who studies plant life

botany study of plant life

cholera disease that causes severe diarrhoea. Sailors in the 17th and 18th centuries often spread deadly cholera to people in faraway lands.

circumnavigate go completely around (circle), especially by water. The HMS *Beagle* set out to circumnavigate Earth.

competition fight for something, such as a needed resource. Competition for food drives evolution.

coral reef warm, clear, shallow ocean habitat that is rich with life. Darwin wrote a book about how coral reefs were formed.

DNA short for "deoxyribonucleic acid", it is the code that forms the basis of life. Parents pass on DNA to their offspring.

descend come from. Humans and chimpanzees descended from a common ape-like ancestor.

dissect take apart. Scientists dissect animals and examine them under a microscope.

diversity difference or variety

economist person who studies how goods and services are shared among a group. Thomas Malthus was an English economist who influenced Darwin.

era period of time. Darwin lived during the Victorian era.

evolution change over time. Darwin found evidence of evolution in the world around him.

fossil remains of a living thing preserved in rock or soil

fossil record record that supports Darwin's theory of change over time

gene sequence of DNA code that controls traits in a living thing. For example, human parents may pass on the gene for green eyes to their child.

geology study of rocks and minerals. Darwin used what he knew about geology to work out how coral reefs formed.

grant money given by the government to a group or individual for a specific purpose. Darwin received a grant to hire experts to study his *Beagle* findings.

habitat where a living thing lives. As cities grow, many animal habitats are shrinking.

Industrial Revolution period that brought great change in technology, such as the growth of railroads, steam ship travel, and factories. The Industrial Revolution took place between 1750 and 1830 in Britain.

infection disease caused by bacteria (germs). Many patients in the early 19th century died of infection after surgery.

majesty term of honour for a queen or king

manual done by hand. Manual labour is done by people, not machines.

marine having to do with the sea. Darwin collected marine animals such as oysters.

mastodon large extinct mammal with big tusks. Mastodons probably looked a lot like elephants.

mentor trusted teacher or guide. Darwin learned a lot from his mentor, John Stevens Henslow.

mutation change. Over time mutations in a species may give rise to a new species.

natural selection process by which useful variations or mutations are selected over time and lead to adaptation

naturalist person who studies nature and living things

organism living thing. Humans are very complex organisms.

origin beginning. Humans and great apes share the same origins.

scarlet fever infection that causes a red rash and sore throat

sloth slow-moving mammal that dwells in the trees. The sloth lives in trees in South America.

specialize change to inhabit a specific area of a habitat. For example, animals may specialize in order to find enough food to survive.

species group of animals with the same characteristics that can mate together and produce offspring. Humans are one species of hominid, a group that includes chimpanzees and gorillas.

specimen sample. Darwin sent back hundreds of specimens on his *Beagle* voyage.

stable fixed or unchanging. Darwin discovered that species are not stable.

sterile free of bacteria; clean. Surgical tools must be sterile or they could cause disease.

taxidermy practice of preparing, stuffing, and mounting dead animals for study or display. Many natural history museums contain displays of taxidermy.

theology study of religion. Darwin studied religion and planned to enter the church.

theory testable scientific explanation that is supported by evidence. Darwin's theory forms the basis of modern science.

variation change in the normal structure of a living thing. Helpful variations in a living thing give it an advantage over its competition.

Want to know more?

Books

Charles Darwin, David C. King (DK Publishing, 2006)

Hobby Guide: The Young Naturalist, A. Mitchell (Usborne Books, 2008)

Inside the Beagle with Charles Darwin, Fiona MacDonald (Enchanted Lion, 2005)

Websites

www.nhm.ac.uk/nature-online/science-of-natural-history

Go to the site of the Natural History Museum and click on "Natural History Biographies" to find information about Darwin. There are also biographies about Wallace and Huxley.

www.bbc.co.uk/history/historic_figures

Click on "D" and then "Charles Darwin" to learn more about him. There are also pages on other well-known naturalists such as Sir Joseph Banks.

Places to visit

Down House

Downe • Kent BR6 7JT • 01689 859119 • www.darwinatdowne.co.uk

Visit the house where Darwin worked on his famous scientific theories. Now an English Heritage site, the house remains very much how it looked when Darwin lived there. See the writing desk where he wrote *On the Origin of Species* and view an exhibition about his life and research. The gardens have been restored and contain orchids and honeybees, just as they did when Darwin lived there in the 1800s.

Galapagos Islands (Ecuador)

Visit the islands that inspired Darwin, lying 966 kilometres (600 miles) off the coast of Ecuador, in the Pacific Ocean. See the tortoises, finches, and other species of animals that inspired Darwin's incredible discoveries. Culpepper Island is now called Darwin Island in honour of Charles Darwin. Fur seals, iguanas, sea lions, dolphins, and many other animals can be found there.

INDEX